Ludwig Aquarius

The dream
and its consequences

This world and the hereafter are a single entity!

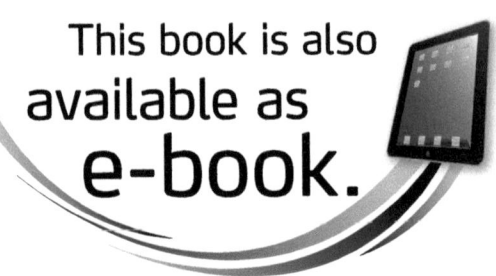

www.novumpublishing.com

All rights of distribution, including via film, radio, and television, photomechanical reproduction, audio storage media, electronic data storage media, and the reprinting of portions of text, are reserved.

© 2021 novum publishing

ISBN 978-3-99107-726-8
Cover and inside illustrations:
Ludwig Aquarius
Cover design, layout & typesetting:
novum publishing

www.novumpublishing.com

Contents

Foreword 7
Fundamental Rights and Freedoms 8
An Unbelievable Experience 9
My Beautiful Faith! 12
A Glimpse into the Beyond 15
D E A T H ? Symbols of Life! 17
The Nucleus 18
The Belief in One God 21
We are free!!! 22
The Last Sermon 25
The Fall of the Gods and Goddesses! 29
Time and Eternity
The Heavenly Perfection 31
The Spiritual-Mental Development 33
Science and Morality 35
The Liberated Woman 37
The Divine Perpetuum Mobile 39
Life! The Inconceivable Miracle! 39
The Four Horsemen of the Apocalypse 41
World Religions 43
The Accuser 45
World Religions, Christianity, Islam, (Judaism)
Waiting for the Messiah since the Beginning 47
The **New** Home! 49
Meditation 51
Epilogue 52

Foreword

I am no theologian. I am by no means a missionary. I am merely recounting personal experiences, which may be taken as a simple narrative. I am at liberty to think critically in this area of tension between religion and my experiences.

We live, thank God, in a time when **freedom of faith and conscience** protects all those who dare to leave the rigid boundaries set by religions. And so, I am able to freely share my experiences that led me naturally to my

beautiful faith.

Ludwig Aquarius

Fundamental Rights and Freedoms

It took quite a long time to give people the foundations for a sensible life in this world. These did not come from God, but from the people, for the people! The horror of World War II created the conditions for this to happen. Nowadays, it would surely be more difficult to achieve this unanimity among nations. It was a learning process that took far too long. Religions could not accept this freedom, because they stood for the opposite. "In thought, word, and deed" encompasses the whole person – both body and soul! A total dictatorship would be inconceivable! Of course, even today, these **fundamental rights and freedoms** have not yet penetrated the minds of everyone; and so, a small, very important selection of them will be given here:

>Freedom of expression
>Freedom of belief and conscience
>Equality before the law
>Freedom of scientific investigation
>Protection of personal liberty
>Protection of the right to life
>Prohibition of torture and slavery

Strangely, these rights established within the framework of the UN are broken by its members on a daily basis. These rights are the iron foundation for a modern life of **responsibility**.

**This responsibility is the cornerstone
of my faith!**

An Unbelievable Experience

Here are some thoughts that may help shed some light on my experience. San Francisco is an incredible melting pot of different faiths, a city where virtually all well-known and lesser-known religions are represented. To list them all would be an arduous undertaking.

I once heard of a church where mediums (seers) came to deliver messages from departed loved ones to the members of that church. It was a church that had a side chapel where pain was alleviated through the laying on of hands. Religious songs were also sung. The most important part of the program, which everyone anxiously awaited, was the **"Messages from the Afterlife!"** There were always four mediums present, who were always changing. Needless to say, that caught my attention. A woman who had recently buried her husband and was eagerly waiting for a sign from him, received an important message: "Unfortunately, I have not made a will, and thus you do not know how to proceed with my inheritance. I shall now give you my will." The wife cried with overwhelming joy and thanked her husband profusely. Naturally, I was skeptical of this message. It could be that this medium was already perfectly familiar with the situation of the family. There was no way for me to verify the truth of the message unless I received a message myself. However, I never received a message, though such messages brought great joy to countless others around me. At the end of an event, I asked a woman who had just worked as a medium to tell me why I never received a message. She looked at me and asked, "Are you a Catholic?" When I answered yes, she said, "You know, Catholics are like rocks!" "So that means I can't expect to receive any messages?" I asked. She replied, "Walk barefoot on the beach where the water is lapping up onto the sand. You lack static electricity!" So, I did just that! Whenever I had time, I went to the beach. Then, curious, I went back to the church. I received my first message that evening! "Your grandfather is here.

He says hello, and that he always loved to sing church hymns." I had no idea which of my grandfathers made himself known in this way. Both were very religious. One was a teacher and played the violin at mass, and the other was a farmer who took part in the first pilgrimage of men from Linz to Jerusalem in 1900. Thus, I needed to ask for clarification. Since my mother had no idea about this strange hobby her father practiced, she asked her sister, who lived with him until his last days. She laughed, and confirmed that he loved to sing church songs, even at home. BINGO! I had found a match, and now knew that my violin-playing grandfather had sent me a message. Only my aunt knew about it. One message worried me tremendously. An uncle – it could only be Uncle Rudolf – said that my mother cured her illnesses with aspirin. However, her current illness could not be cured with that medicine. I immediately investigated and received some relieving news – she was suffering from extremely high blood pressure. She was already receiving medical treatment. They didn't want me to worry unnecessarily. They had no idea that a worried soul had notified me from the afterlife! I had received several messages before the most wonderful one came: "Your father is here!" I can still feel the elation of my soul today! "He says you are deeply worried about finding a job. You don't have to worry, in two weeks the problem will be solved." I was totally blown away! My beloved father was still worried about me!

I had myself evaluated, because I was unable to work in my profession. The test did not turn up particularly positive results. I was classified as a perfectionist. A Carinthian who had trained as a car painter in Austria was hired and fired within a week. He could not understand why; after all, his work was substantially better than that of his colleagues. He simply couldn't see how to get his feet on the ground. One day he ran into a former co-worker and lamented his misfortune. The co-worker laughed and said: "While you were painting 2 cars, I was doing 3! Good grief, the boss's cash register has to keep ringing!" His next job turned into a permanent one! So, I was perfect and simply had bad prospects.

What a coincidence! A private rescue company showed interest in me and took me on, with the following conditions: "You start tomorrow at 8 o'clock with no beard and with a license for rescue vehicles." My God, I had a job where perfect people were needed.

The driver's license office is open all day, since Americans have to take an exam every three years, with the option to choose the date. I immediately got the paperwork, got in my passenger car and 'studied' for the test. I went to the exam and passed. In the evening, I shaved my beard, which caused my sweetheart to tear up. After all, she had only ever known me with a beard. The next day, I reported for duty at 8 o'clock sharp. It had not yet been two weeks. My father gave me the necessary support and confidence. Could I still have any objections and doubts? When I left for home three years later, I received probably the rarest job reference you can get. It promised that I would be taken back at any time, should I wish to do so.

My Beautiful Faith!

I was living overseas and dreaming about my non-existent house, which was full of my non-existent paintings.

I had neither that house nor the ability to create these paintings. However, I was completely convinced that this house and the paintings were real.

When I awoke, I decided to start the journey home to fulfill this dream. However, I was not financially able to realize my dream. I also had no idea how to paint these unique pictures. It took twenty years to build. Once the basement was finished, my wife and I moved in to avoid having to pay rent. This basement apartment is still very much appreciated today. During this long time, I experimented to find a suitable painting surface. I finally found it. Now I had to work out a suitable painting technique. I had no idea what subjects to paint. I had already come so far in realizing my dream that I was ready to clear the last hurdle.

I primed my canvas with white paint and placed it in front of me. I studied the surface for some time. Suddenly, I began to see very fine lines. I painted them out and kept looking. That is how my first painting came into being. This method was the key to my paintings, which all made sense. It became clear to me that the subject giver from beyond supported me in this world! **This world and the world of the hereafter merged into one! I had found my beautiful faith!**

Our vibrant world: people, animals and plants belong together! This life, this divine breath, encompasses all life forms of the universe, both in this world and the hereafter. Life cannot be destroyed. Birth and death are merely transitions! The often-asked question "How could God allow this?" is only relevant to us. To God, we are not lost! This wondrous life embedded in the divine breath of eternal life is the most glorious realization that speaks from my pictures. There are no punishments! **There is only learning!** It is up to man to reach the highest level of **human existence** and defeat the animal within. There is no fear. There are no punishments!

Abandon all your addictions and set yourself free! Let your soul fly and ascend above your – inner animal – to the highest level of bliss: being human! This is the knowledge that my otherworldly teacher gave me through my paintings. It is with gratitude that I remain connected to him.

A Glimpse into the Beyond

I wished for a glimpse into the other world. I primed the painting surface with white and painted a curtain that was open from the center to be able to look through. I concentrated now on the center of the canvas for my painting. I desperately wanted to look into the beyond! However, all I could see was the white canvas. But I did not give up. Suddenly, I saw very delicate lines and began to paint them. A strange figure emerged, which seemed to be made up of the bodies of several animals. A bright, broken ribbon was connected to it. I had a beginning and hoped to find out more. Faces began to appear, at which point I painted and painted enthusiastically. Finally, a flying bird also emerged. I stood the painting up to explore its meaning.

Explanation: the prominent figure in the center represents the **animal world**. The broken ribbon embodies the **plant world**, which forms a hurdle. This hurdle has been overcome by the upper three faces. Their facial expressions with closed eyes show serenity and exude inner peace. The goal has been achieved! The lower faces express great disappointment. You have arrived at reality. They have not been able to detach themselves from the animal world in this world in order to develop into true "human beings". There's more to a human being than simply satisfying basic needs. The animal world does that too. Only we humans are selected and enabled to reach the highest consecrations; not only the animal world watches over it, but also the divine breath in the form of a white dove!

Self-knowledge recognizes immediately which deficiencies one has accumulated in this world, which must be worked off in order to also be allowed to enter into Bliss. We teach ourselves the lessons! And yet, the picture reveals nothing about where we have to work through this task. There are no punishments. Hell, and purgatory are merely instruments of power used by religious dictatorships to ruin this world for people. There is only one commandment: Responsibility for all actions!

DEATH?
Symbols of Life!

The inevitability of death seems to weigh heavily on the poor sinner. He faces the sacrificial bowl in front of him, and in the background, the common symbolic figure. Of course, the dying man does not realize that he isn't going to lose his life altogether. This fear, which is clearly recognizable, is about hell and purgatory. He doesn't even dare to think about paradise, because it has been drilled into him all his life by the priests of his religion: "The road to hell is paved with good intentions", He has failed again and again with his good intentions. He tried hard and yet he did not reach the goal he had set.

I have a very interesting encyclopedia that explains very nicely the symbols created in paintings from all over the world.

Symbols: The **peacock** sitting on his right shoulder is a symbol of life.

The **snake**, prominently depicted, bears the reputation of eternal youth due to its shedding of skin.

Jesus redeemed from the terrible torments extends his arms up in the air!

In the lower area one sees a **seed** from the plant world which represents the newly germinating life.

Conclusion: the human, animal, and plant worlds are clearly represented. The fear of the human being is completely unfounded, because he crosses completely painlessly to meet his own self. Either he manages to overcome the hurdle waiting for him through his responsible humanity or he starts to work off his future tasks. This world and the next world are just the two sides of the divine coin!

I ask all Christians who pray the Creed with conviction to refrain from reading this following chapter. I am no theologian or missionary. The basic right of the free expression allows me to write this contribution!

The Nucleus

At first, I could not understand the role of Jesus in the picture. Jesus, freed from the torments, raises his arms in the air! Death was so close that he even damaged the sacrificial bowl.

Since I am a descendant of primates, not of Adam and Eve, I can also see the Christian history of salvation, with which I was brought up, with different eyes! Of course, I deal only with my own view and have no evidence whether my reasoning is correct.

He damaged the sacrificial bowl but did not accept it. He wasn't yet ready to lose his earthly life!

Then I read the following account in a book titled **No and Amen** by Mrs. Uta Ranke-Heinemann, professor of Catholic theology: "It is reported by a man named Joseph of Arimathea that he took the body of Jesus from the cross. With the help of Nicodemus, who had brought a mixture of one hundred pounds of myrrh and aloe (Joh. 19,39), which is an enormous amount of about 33 kilograms (1 pound = 1 Roman libra = 327.45 g), he wrapped Jesus together with these spices in a linen cloth and laid him in a new tomb in a garden at the place of his execution, because of the Jews' preparation day and because the tomb was nearby (Joh. 29,42).

Now I suddenly understood my picture. They laid the dead Jesus in these **medicinal herbs: Myrrh** – which is disinfecting, astringent, promotes scarring, and is styptic.

Aloe – a pharmaceutical drug and anti-inflammatory!

One can thus see the history of Jesus' suffering in a completely new light. I simply stay on the ground and remove the **miracles** from the terrible events. In order to save Jesus from an unjust death, a top-secret agreement was made:

Pilate ("I see no fault in him!")

Joseph of Arimathea (Pharisee and high judge)

Nicodemus (Pharisee and high judge who procured the healing herbs)

agreed on a deal that the crucifixion must take place very late on **Friday** to shorten the time on the cross for Jesus. After all, the Sabbath begins on Friday evening. At that time, no condemned person is allowed to hang on the cross. The two condemned men next to Jesus were taken down alive and killed by breaking their bones. Jesus' death was verified by the lance thrust on the **right** side of his chest and reported to Pilate. Of course, the soldier's lance could only cause a non-threatening flesh wound, since Jesus was too high up on the cross. It could not wound any vital organ. He was declared dead. His bones were therefore not broken. **The deal would have failed otherwise!** Jesus, who was in deep unconsciousness, was carefully removed and wrapped in a cloth (shroud in Turin). In the cave tomb that was prepared, he was wrapped in the healing herbs and transported during the night for further medical treatment. Pilate had made sure, together with his soldiers, that there were no witnesses at the time of removal. Thus, the tomb was empty in the morning! After three days, there were only external injuries, he had recovered so much that he could show himself to his disciples. They now regarded him as having performed a great miracle, since they and even Jesus had no idea about the deal that was made! The miracle of the resurrection had come true! Of course, during those three days Jesus was enlightened about his salvation and the consequences that came as a result. He had to protect his saviors at all costs and leave the country. All appearances had to be regarded as miracles. This was not difficult for him, as many a miracle was said to have been performed by him. The cunning stunt had worked out perfectly!!

Jesus left his disciples and set out for Kashmir. On this way he happened to meet **Saul,** who was on his way to Damascus to persecute the Christians there. Jesus asked him the famous question, "Saul, why are you persecuting me?" One cannot imagine the horror this man felt. The crucified rebel was standing before him **in the flesh**! This miracle turned him into Paul! This man's fanaticism was the **nucleus** for Christianity that he carried out into the world. Had it not been for this man, we would never have heard of the itinerant preacher Jesus. Even the terrible acts that have happened in his name throughout history would never have taken place!

Thank God I descend from primates!

Books: "Jesus Lived and Died in Kashmir" by Andreas Faber-Kaiser.
"Did Jesus Die in Kashmir?" by Siegfried Obermeier

Note: Jesus never intended to establish a world religion. He even forbade his disciples to go to the heathens! They should **only** take care of the lost sheep of the house of Israel (Matth. 9.36-10.8)! Paul was not a disciple and apparently did not feel bound by this prohibition Jesus had made! Actually, from today's point of view, it is completely irrelevant whether my view of the events is right or wrong! It was science that pulled the ground out from below Christianity! The world was not created in seven days! For example, the author had no knowledge of the dinosaurs that roamed the Earth many millions of years ago. However, it is really all just a metaphor. The Bible Belt in the USA believes that the Bible only contains facts. Evolution is not allowed to be taught at all. Why do people believe in old books that no longer correspond to the knowledge of today in any way? Christianity, of course, clings to this world that it has formed over thousands of years. Today, however, many church customs have become tourist events. After all, no one today believes that the Corpus Christi Day lake festivals of Hallstatt and Traunkirchen are religious events to strengthen people's faith. They are merely spectacles that must be experienced. Of course, this also applies to all secular events. The economy can no longer do without them. Anyone who believes that religions cannot perish should go to Egypt and admire the mighty testimonies of a religion that has simply disappeared! Many people visit churches and monasteries today without spiritual edification. They go simply to appreciate the artistic value! It is time for a break-up!

The Belief in One God

We now find ourselves with the God of the chosen people, who **jealously watches** over the Israelite tribes and makes sure that only he is worshiped by his people. There were still other gods present. Therefore, he is not at all omnipotent.

Only the members of this population were involved in the emergence of Christianity. It is natural that they took **their** god with them into the new teaching. Jesus is the son of their God, but he was not recognized by the tribes as the Messiah.

When science began to look at the evolution of all life forms, they found the **ape** to be the natural predecessor of man. The beautiful edifice of our common primordial parents came crashing down! But for the chosen people, everything remained as it always was common primordial parents (Adam and Eve), common original sin passed down by their primordial parents, strict regulations on how to live imposed by their God, with the mission to subjugate the Earth. Their God chose **them** and not **U S !!!**

Right at this time, the Christians should have realized that they had been **usurping** the god of a certain people for millennia without a second thought! So, as science has proven, we descended from the apes. This realization must lead to consequences: there is no **original sin**! We have no **primordial parents** who have sinned against God! We have no **orders** to enslave the earth. Religious means of holding power (the devil, hell, purgatory etc.), which have frightened and still frighten believers, were not **invented by the apes!!!**

We are free!!!

What a glorious feeling! We have the almighty, all-embracing, all-pervading **GOD**, whose dominion reaches to the farthest galaxies!!! He gives us a completely free hand in all domains of life. He readily permits the catastrophes of nature and those of man! He makes both the microcosm and macrocosm available to be freely explored! Ethics seems to have no influence on the law of cause and effect. Humans can build and they can destroy. They may cherish or consume the earth, the basis of our life. It is our **sole responsibility** to educate people who are capable of proving themselves **worthy** of the Almighty's generosity. **Freedom without responsibility** means: C H A O S !

I have therefore arrived at home from a foreign land!!!

May Jesus forgive me. I will adapt his famous prayer for my own use:

Our Father, who are in heaven,	Almighty!
Hallowed be thy name.	Holy is thy name
Thy Kingdom come.	Your kingdom is here!
Thy will be done,	Thy will is done!
On Earth as it is in heaven.	Give all humans their daily bread.
Give us this day our daily bread.	Forgive us our trespasses,
And forgive us our trespasses,	You lead us not into temptation.
As we forgive those that trespass	For thine is the kingdom, the power and
And lead us not into temptation,	the glory forever and ever.
But deliver us from evil.	Amen.
For thine is the kingdom, the power and the glory forever.	
Amen.	

Explanation: God is omnipotent. This omnipotence eliminates its local limitation. Holy means his name is unknown. This omnipotence prevents even God himself from renouncing his will. Renouncing it would also be an expression of his will. His will is therefore all-embracing! All humans need their daily bread! The forgiving of guilt cannot be limited by our sad ability to forgive! We would look very bad. Temptation is impossible by his omnipotence, because he knows the outcome. The conclusion is actually not necessary, because he does not need our confirmation!

Of course, Jesus taught us the "Lord's Prayer" correctly. He prayed to his God, after all!

P.S.: Just think of Abraham, who was to prove his love for God through the cruel murder of his own son.

The Last Sermon

People have passed by his chapel for thousands of years, following one order:

Subjugate the Earth!

The order should be considered as over-fulfilled. His sermons had caused great fear. They were about hell, devils, witches, purgatory and the very narrow path to Heaven, which only a select few may walk. The path past the chapel emptied out. Nature was of no concern and has died out. There is desolation! Modern people could do nothing with the sermons. They have the basic rights and freedoms in their bags, which are applicable to all people in order for them to be able to live a life with freedom and responsibility!

Subjugate the Earth!

The Earth isn't subjugated today – it is enslaved! The God of the Bible did not foresee the terrible consequences of his command! Let us ask the young people who founded "Fridays for Future" whether they obey or reject this command, which is still written in the Bible today! The words of God cannot be changed! They are set in stone!

When I think of my youth, I start to reminisce. The war couldn't destroy nature. We had meadows of flowers filled with butterflies and shiny beetles. We could catch crayfish in clean streams and fish without permission. Women washed their clothes in the clear water. The birds chirped and eagerly cared for their offspring. Other natural scenes could be found everywhere. Today, every small garden has an "English lawn", which is mowed every week, bringing with it the noise and stench of riding lawn mowers. The shrubs must be trimmed. Every unwanted little flower is obliterated with chemicals. Insects have disappeared, and with them the birds, as they can no longer feed their nestlings. Yes, even the smallest spot of the garden is subjugated by us!

Yesterday I was delighted to see two butterflies (cabbage-white butterflies) on their nuptial flight. They were persecuted like pests in my youth. Today, a rare appearance by these creatures gives me great joy!

We had everything and we went by foot! The elite had bicycles and the peasants had their horse-drawn carts. This world is lost, of course, and the highly necessary alternatives are sought.

Each parish had a pastor (preacher). Nowadays. parishes are being merged together as many people have moved on. In Germany, churches are being sold, because no one wants to pay for their upkeep. They are now being expanded and used privately for all sorts of purposes.

Apparently, nature is not the only one singing its swan song!!!

This world and the hereafter are a single entity!

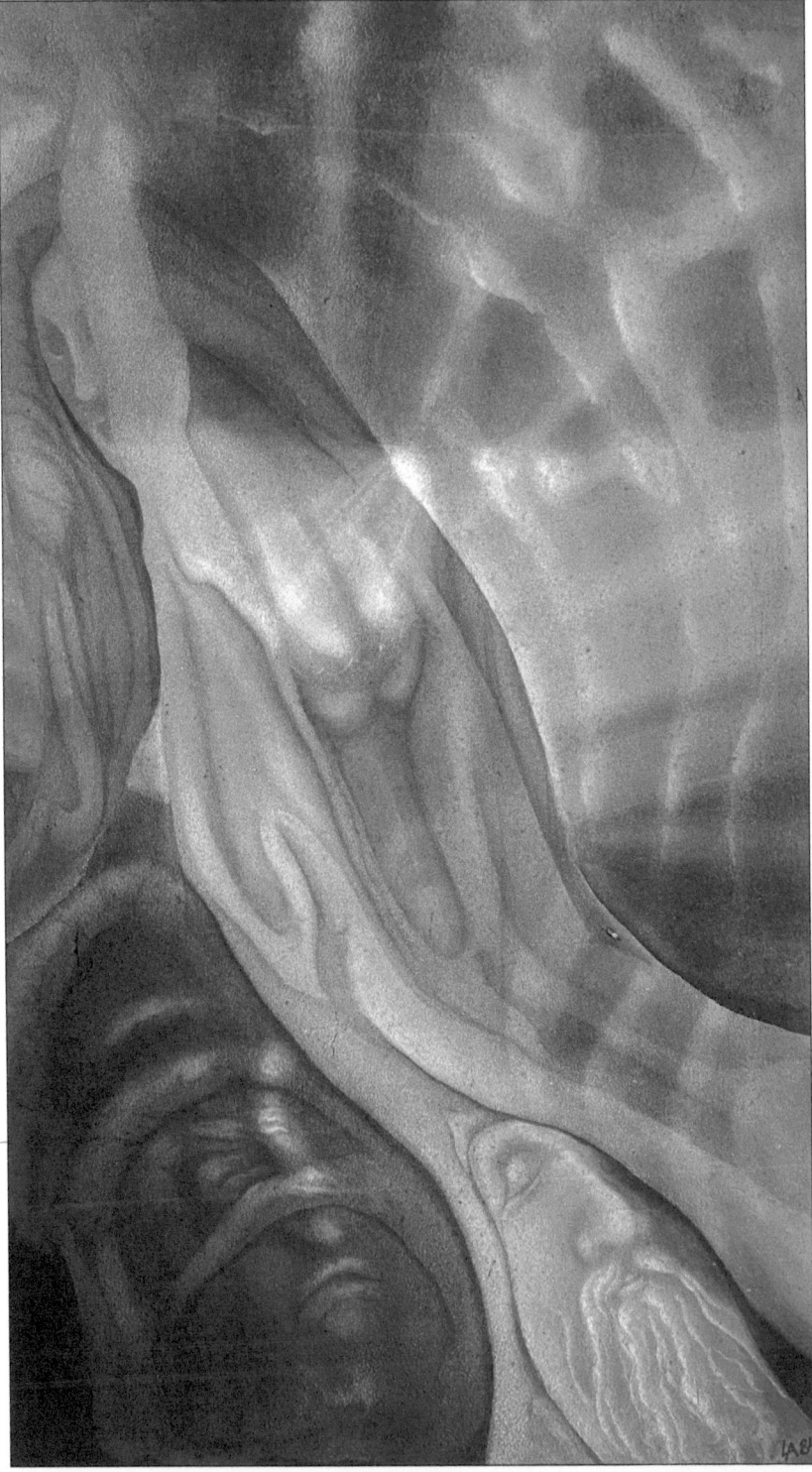

The Fall of the Gods and Goddesses!

Man **thought up** the goddesses and gods and their warriors defended them. Some also believe in space travelers who were technically far superior to humans. Be it as it may! In the field of morality, they weren't! That's what the myths say.

Emptying the heaven in order to reach the One-God-Faith was successfully carried out by Christianity. There was now enough space created to fill it with tens of thousands of saints. The gods and goddesses were able to help people **directly**. Saints, however, must put in a **good word** with God for their supplicants! Corruption also seems to play a role with this God. Somehow, he can hear better when the request is made by a saint.

There is an old saying, **"Help yourself, and God will help you!" Now we have arrived at the Almighty!**

He gives you the freedom of choice. However, He does not free you from the **responsibility** to always determine your actions! We have arrived in the whimsical, factual, modern life, the blueprint of which must comprise the fundamental rights and freedoms.

THANK GOD!

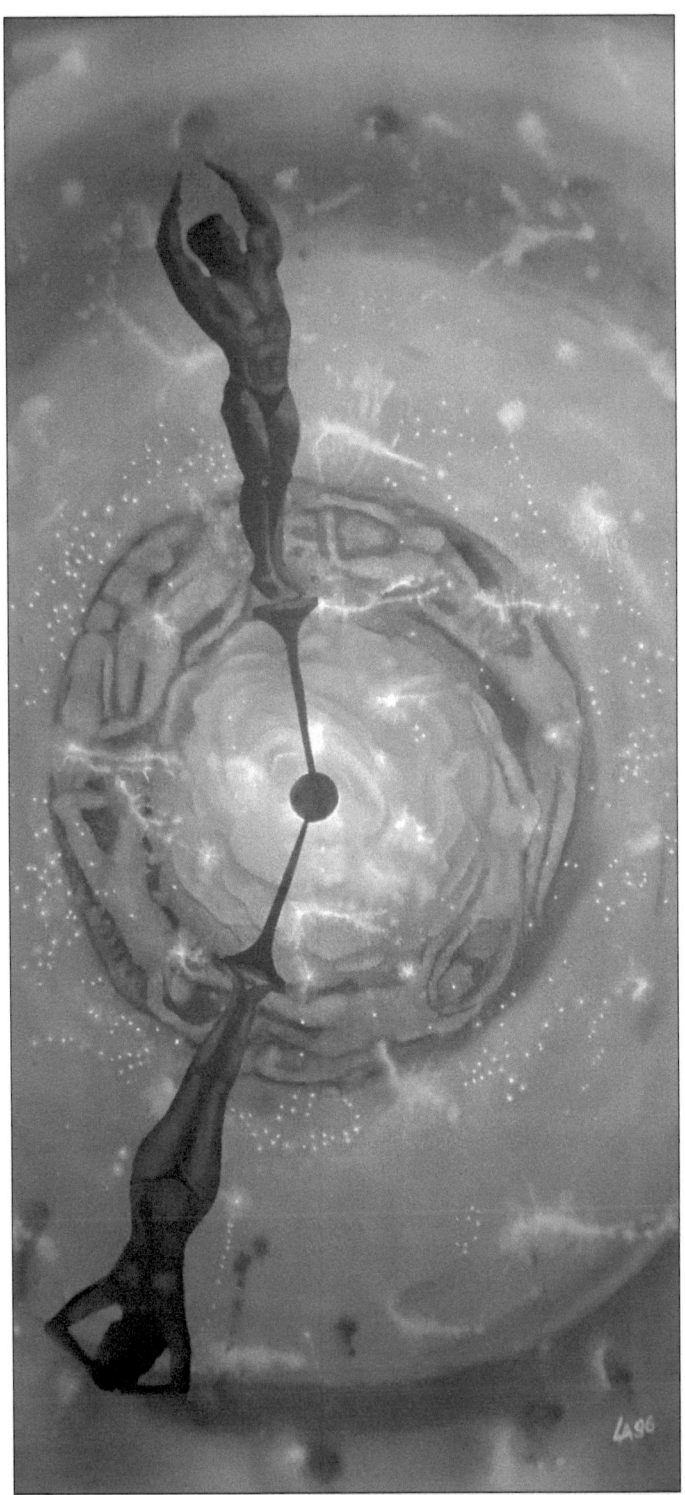

Time and Eternity
The Heavenly Perfection

Man and woman are bound by time in this world. Their time is irrevocably running out. Scientists are working to extend rich people's lives accordingly. Immortality is a goal that will never be reached. It is the fear of death, whose shrouds have no pockets. Ancient cultures solved this problem with valuable burial objects. Today, however, we are only concerned with this world, which we try to hold onto with all our might, as we know that such burial objects are of no use in the afterlife. Even rich people will have to ask themselves once they get there, "How did I use my wealth to achieve my **humanity**?" Living the good life alone is certainly not enough. When the Vatican was built, people were allowed to shorten their time in purgatory or even buy their way into heaven by making financial contributions. This possibility no longer exists either. Heaven is open to all people who have reached the given goal of **humanity**. Modern enlightened man knows his **responsibility**, which he owes to God's work of creation.

Note: The heavenly rose also appears in literature, as I was pleased to discover after completing the painting. It is the symbol of human perfection!

The Spiritual-Mental Development

1. Realization: Since man, as we know from science, is descended from the apes, he is a fixed part of nature and not a special creation of a god. He is so deeply rooted in the animal world that he knows the advantages of the other animals very well and believes that he can acquire them through masks. He sees the animal and plant world as his livelihood. Plants have green leaves, which are upright and strong! The divine law of cause and effect has made his mental development possible. To understand the inexplicable phenomena of nature, he invented higher beings (gods and goddesses), which he sought to appease with offerings.

2. Realization: He could pass on the knowledge gained to the next generation. It was through this that the ape evolved into a human being! Each generation was able to build on the experience and knowledge of the ancestors and thus laid the foundations for the sciences! The ibis was the symbol for science in Egypt, its wings also touching primitive man. The chest of the scientist depicts the universe. Nature begins to weaken because of the constant interventions of man. The leaves of the plant no longer possess their original strength. Man has shamelessly exploited nature and its wealth.

3. Realization: Religions have often opposed scientific knowledge with all their might, because their faith could not keep up with progress. That wasn't going to work in the long run. Heaven and hell are left for the priests! Modern people are unable to do anything with these old terms anymore!

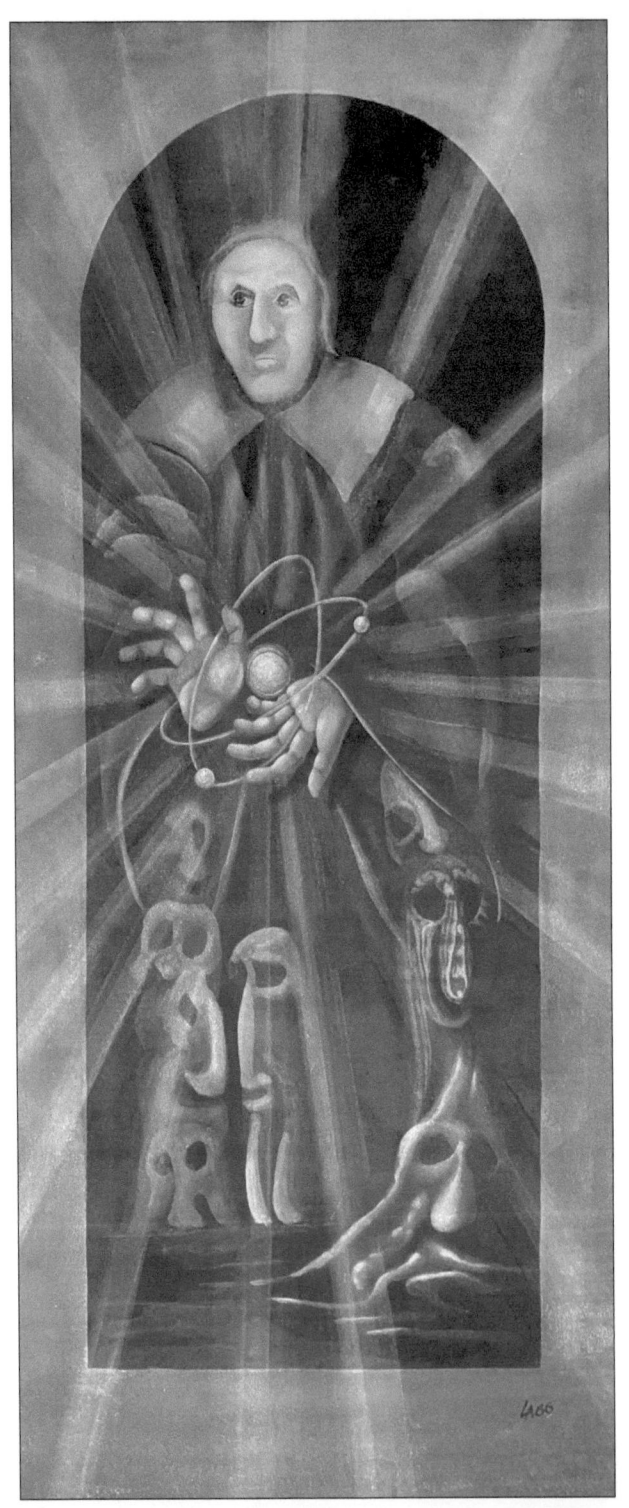

Science and Morality

Man, in his unrestrained urge to discover, is increasingly coming into conflict with ethics. However, countries are very different when it comes to their interpretation. Christian ethics even play very different roles in Christian countries. Discovery of the tremendous power of the atom didn't first result in dangerous power plants, but rather the **atomic bomb**! It killed an enormous number of people who weren't even soldiers! The survivors were immediately examined to enrich medical knowledge. The military always observes all scientific works to increase their potential to destroy. The vaunted safety of nuclear power plants has taken a huge hit with the horrific accidents at Chernobyl, Harrisburg, and Fukushima. Science continues to research. Industry is also self-interested and has no moral qualms about maximizing profits. After all, the well-known maxim holds true all too often: profits are privatized, and losses are socialized!

This picture shows the scientist how his discoveries also bring dangerous effects that strike fear in the hearts of many!

There is only one commandment: **To be responsible for all actions!**

The Liberated Woman

How wonderful is it to see our women free to engage in all kinds of activities that were once reserved only for men? Although this is largely thanks to enlightened men who created the legal conditions for liberation. Throughout its long history, the Christian religion has been a veritable disaster for the female believers. Thousands were cruelly tortured as witches over the centuries and burned alive to snatch prey from the devil. Even today, women are still dealt a rather poor hand in the church as an institution. They are more or less tolerated as an auxiliary.

Democracy is a disaster for the hierarchical structure of the church. The systems no longer fit together. The result of this development can already be foreseen.

But a socially liberated woman must also liberate herself **spiritually**. She must question everything that has been imparted to her in the course of her religious life and that weighs on her conscience. **She is now fully responsible for her actions!** Consider a church wedding, in which the bride and groom swear allegiance to each other for the rest of their lives. "What God has joined, man must not separate!" However, the priest and the bride and groom know that life today is viewed in stages, and divorce is always left open as an option. We must not deceive ourselves! Modern man needs clarity and truth. This is the only basis on which we can build a reasonable life.

Picture: Today **our woman** stands proudly, naked, with both legs firmly on our earth, which has entrusted her with the most outstanding task of being a mother! A great number of women, enslaved by religions, are still waiting for their liberation! The fundamental rights and liberties must be finally implemented for all people.

Note: The green color connects all women of the world with Mother Earth!

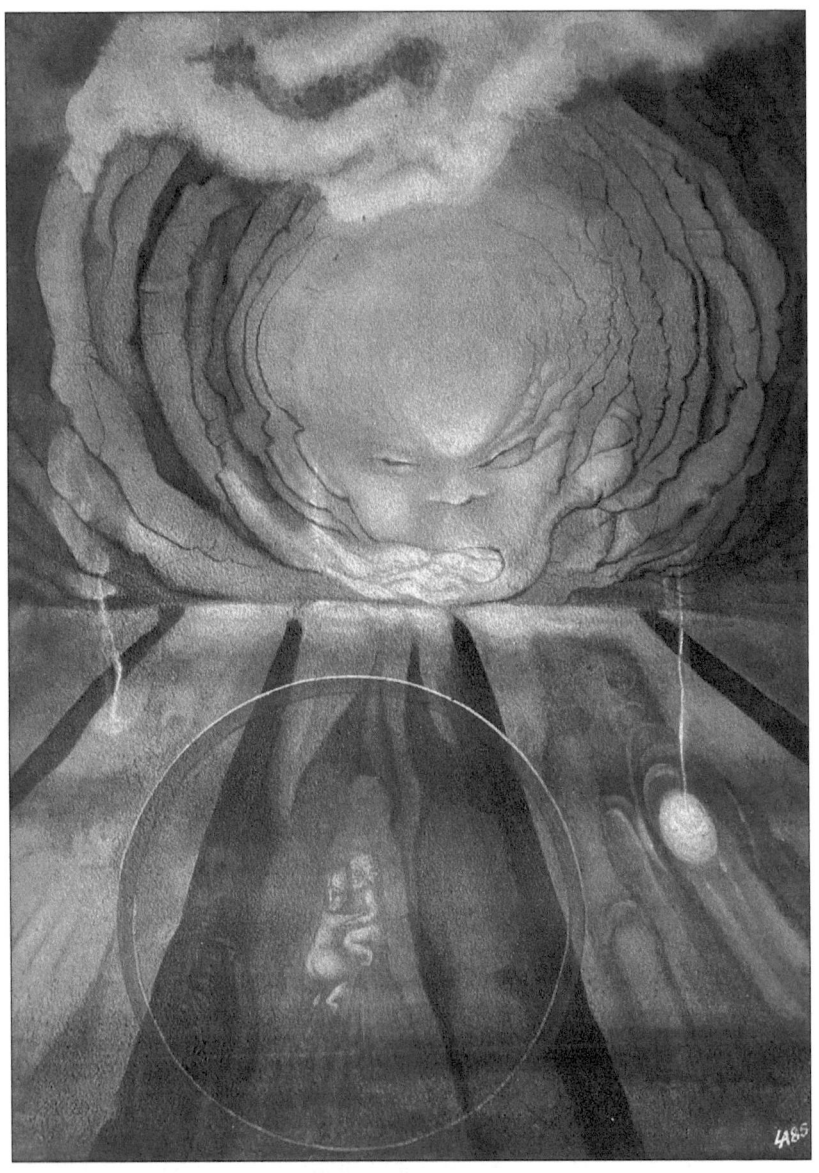

The Divine Perpetuum Mobile

Life! The Inconceivable Miracle!

The divine wheel of becoming and passing uninterruptedly turns! It represents the change from this world to the next world and vice versa! This process encompasses the entirety of life in nature. People, viewed under a magnifying glass, experience the **fear of death** and do not know that life is the **spark** of the **Almighty**, and thus can never come into danger! If two people really love each other from the heart, their connection remains from this world to the beyond! They continue to feel the nearness of their beloved soul!

One can rightly say, "Love kills death!".

The Four Horsemen of the Apocalypse

When the first privately built rocket brought two astronauts to the ISS, everybody heard the news! The current president of the great country exclaimed enthusiastically, "We will now have the most powerful weapons in the world!" China is also suspected of having triggered the coronavirus pandemic through an oversight in bio-weapons production.

This Christian country also had no inhibitions during World War II to end the war by dropping two atomic bombs on the civilian population of the enemy! The catastrophic and enthusiastic exclamation of the president is therefore no joke, but rather a dire omen for vast swaths of mankind!

The apocalypse has nothing to do with God. It is the horrible act of man against man. After the U.S. coped with the bombs without major problems, the Bible, which the president likes to hold up with such pride, will also help them with the apocalypse. The whole country talks about **Jesus** constantly; their incredibly rich preachers fill huge churches promising unlimited happiness in the name of Jesus! For hours, the name of Jesus is invoked, while the preachers line their pockets. With their wealth, they also show that Jesus has also granted them access to the most modern private airplanes, which they operate on their large estates. Since they need all their wealth to take care of their religious followers, they don't need to pay taxes either!

In every election, there are supplementary questions to answer. One question asked in the seventies was, "Do you think it is right that rich people should pay more taxes?" This question was answered with a resounding no! I expected a different answer, but instead was quickly answered with, "Once I'm rich, I certainly won't want to pay higher taxes!"!

So, the horsemen of the apocalypse are not sent by God, even if the seven seals fly from the scroll, but rather by irresponsible people themselves!

**Man should have never found the FLINT,
because progress and weapons go together until today!!**

World Religions

Every religion preaches peace! Unfortunately, each also has its own God, and the right one! All other people are infidels and must be either converted or killed. The peace-loving religions become murdering hordes if they meet the competition. The history books are full of their misdeeds. When secessions occur, the old cruelty resurfaces. A few days ago in Baghdad, a Sunite cab driver cut off the head of a Shiite boy next to his mother with a shard of glass! He believes that he will be rewarded for this act by his God! The West, under the leadership of Big Brother, does not employ any angels of peace either. Religion also plays a very large role in their ranks! When will it finally succeed in instilling the **fundamental rights and liberties** adopted by the UN for the whole world into the brains of the people?! It doesn't matter at all what somebody believes. Of course, when you look around, the remnants of the Middle Ages can still be felt. It is high time to put them to rest! That applies to all people in this big village of ours!

The picture detail shows a desperate woman who still wants to save **life** amidst total annihilation! The religions grow out of the barren soil and capture in this way the great mass of people who are always in the struggle of life! They confidently expect help from **above** which is promised to them by the priests if they behave humbly.

The Accuser

In all wars and similar conflicts, the majority of women are among the victims of the men on the opposite side. The world of women is not that of the battle axe. Women are, by nature, committed to life! They want to preserve life, which suddenly has no more value and is savagely destroyed! Their voices are not heard! They have to endure. They are, to this day, an essential part of the spoils of war for the victors, with all the terrible consequences this entails! Her love of peace is far more advanced than that of men. Only the fundamental rights and liberties can prevent the disaster. Women and children need special protection! A woman in uniform is an exaggeration of equality! Nature has not intended them for it!

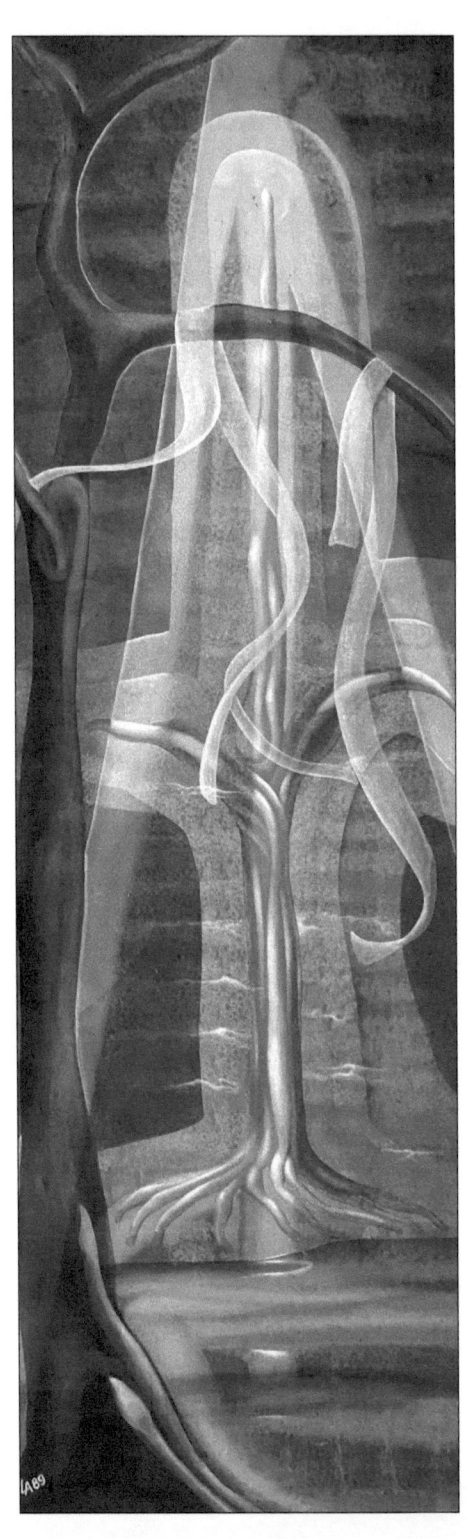

World Religions

Christianity

Islam

(Judaism)

Waiting for the

Messiah since the Beginning

It was not worth waiting for him. He simply did not come. Many people still can't believe it, even though he missed many appointments throughout history. Even his disciples believed in his imminent return. After two thousand years, he still hasn't appeared! The Messiah is not coming! The wait is finally over! He will not ride down from heaven on a white horse and save the world. Nor will He rule the world from Jerusalem for a long time. The dead will not rise from their graves, because they are certainly not to be found there.

    The picture shows the Earth as it appears to man when saved through the miracle of the Messiah. Dead snakes. From the dead tree, ribbons blow in the wind, which with some imagination reveal the IHS Christogram. Who must save the earth? It is us!!!

The New Home!

Where are the virgin planets waiting for us to exploit them? The Earth is exploited and can no longer feed the great mass of people. A third of mankind must die, said a revered American politician. Pandemics are certainly warmly welcomed for this reason!

The elites are excited by the advancement in rocket technology because it offers the possibility of escape from this overpopulated Earth.

Only more comfortable, safer spaceships need to be built. Astronomers are scouring the universe day and night with huge telescopes! And why wouldn't we make it? After all, UFOs have come here!

I wish our elites will have a safe journey, not simply because they are leaving me! Along with them, wars will disappear, and **fundamental rights and freedoms** will fully come into effect. **Social security** must be introduced **worldwide** to limit large families to two children! The **education system** must be **mandatory and open** to all people! **Democracy** must be declared the only permitted form of government. The **UN** must become a committee of **equal** states, which adopts peaceful **majority decisions** for the well-being of all mankind. All warfare systems and bombs shall be banned and destroyed!

We will reclaim our glorious home, the blue planet, with reason and **responsibility**! **"Fridays for Future"** is a beginning!

Meditation

Meditation is the extraordinary medium to feel the closeness of the beyond. It helps to fill this world with the joy of being alive, and to experience the unity of the two worlds without fear. This alone is the goal of my meditation!

Epilogue

It would be a most glorious endeavor for theologians of all religions to come together in order to compare their beliefs without prejudice, in which general validity can be attained. How often does one hear the desperate saying: "When I return to this world, I will…!"

This saying is accepted by all people – including Christians! – without any problems, although it is a principle of Buddhism. People who claim to have been in this world once before were able to describe their former place of existence and find it again. Such rediscovery has already been depicted on television. This non-contentious, honest discussion can lead to a generally accepted world religion, which would prevent all religiously enforced wars. Peaceful coexistence could be achieved in one fell swoop. One could speak of a real **salvation**! An infinite number of people would breathe a sigh of relief, exclaiming, **"Thank God, the chaos and hatred are over!"** You may, of course, guess which God I am talking about. We may project all good qualities to the highest perfection onto this all-embracing, all-pervading Being and envelop ourselves in His infinite goodness. The only commandment is to **learn and take responsibility** in order to reach the highest level of human existence. Let us throw into the fire of oblivion all the junk piled up from ancient times (hell, the devil, purgatory, sins, etc.), which has caused so many people fear and terror in the most evil form! I am not speaking of the Father. I am speaking of the **Supreme Being**, who permeates all of our fibers. Let us free ourselves and go on the most satisfying journey of discovery within **ourselves.**

I would, however, like to repeat what I said in the foreword:

I am no theologian. I am by no means a missionary. I am not a medium (seer). I simply speak of my own personal experiences, which may be taken as a humble narrative. I am at liberty to think in this area of tension between religion and my experiences.

We live, thank God, in a time when freedom of faith and conscience protects all those who dare to leave the strongly circumscribed field of religions. And so, I can freely share my experiences that led me naturally to my

beautiful faith.

Ludwig Aquarius

Rate this book on our website!

www.novumpublishing.com

novum 🕮 PUBLISHER FOR NEW AUTHORS

The publisher

> *He who stops getting better stops being good.*

This is the motto of novum publishing, and our focus is on finding new manuscripts, publishing them and offering long-term support to the authors.
Our publishing house was founded in 1997, and since then it has become THE expert for new authors and has won numerous awards.

Our editorial team will peruse each manuscript within a few weeks free of charge and without obligation.

You will find more information about
novum publishing and our books on the internet:

w w w . n o v u m p u b l i s h i n g . c o m